CONSTITUTION

AND

BY-LAWS

OF THE

New Orleans Academy of Sciences:

TOGETHER WITH A LIST OF

FELLOWS,

HONORARY, AND CORRESPONDING MEMBERS.

NEW ORLEANS:
TRUE DELTA JOB OFFICE, 18 ST. CHARLES STREET.
1859.

NOTE.

[PART I of the First Volume of the TRANSACTIONS OF THE NEW ORLEANS ACADEMY OF SCIENCES, has been sent to all the kindred Institutions with which this Academy corresponds, both in Europe and America.

The subsequent Transactions will also be forwarded as soon as published, together with other publications of the Academy.

The Academy solicits in exchange the publications of other Societies ; also contributions to its Scientific Museum.]

CONSTITUTION

AND

BY-LAWS

OF THE

New Orleans Academy of Sciences:

TOGETHER WITH A LIST OF

FELLOWS,

HONORARY, AND CORRESPONDING MEMBERS.

NEW ORLEANS:
TRUE DELTA JOB OFFICE, 18 ST. CHARLES STREET.
1859.

NEW-ORLEANS ACADEMY OF SCIENCES.
1853.

OFFICERS FOR 1859.

PRESIDENT :

PROF. J. L. RIDDELL, A. M., M. D.

VICE PRESIDENTS :

J. S. COPES, M. D. WM. B. LINDSAY, M. D.

CORRESPONDING SECRETARY :

PROF. A. VALLAS.

RECORDING SECRETARY ;

NOAH B. BENEDICT, M. D.

REGISTRAR :

JAMES B. DURAND.

TREASURER :

JAMES K. BAILEY.

LIBRARIAN :

R. C. KERR.

CURATORS :

DR. J. S. KNAPP, HENRY CLINE.

CHAIRMEN OF SCIENTIFIC SECTIONS, 1859–60.

I.
NATURAL HISTORY OF ANIMALS,
DR. T. G. RICHARDSON.

II.
BOTANY,
PROF. J. L. RIDDELL.

III.
GEOLOGY AND MINERALOGY,
P. H. SKIPWITH, ESQ.

IV.
CHEMISTRY AND NATURAL PHILOSOPHY,
PROF. I. L. CRAWCOUR.

V.
ASTRONOMY AND MATHEMATICS,
PROF. A. VALLAS.

VI.
ANTIQUARIAN RESEARCHES AND ETHNOLOGY,
DR. J. S. COPES.

VII.
HISTORY AND BIOGRAPHY,
HON. CHARLES GAYARRE.

VIII.
PHILOLOGY,
PROF. JOHN MACNAIR.

IX.
MEDICINE AND PHYSIOLOGY,
DR. N. B. BENEDICT.

X.
GEOGRAPHY, STATISTICS AND METEOROLOGY,
PROF. J. D. B. DEBOW.

XI.
PSYCHOLOGY AND ÆESTHETICS,
DR. SAMUEL A. CARTWRIGHT.

XII.
AGRICULTURE,
DR. W. B. LINDSAY.

XIII.
JURISPRUDENCE AND POLITICAL ECONOMY,
P. E. BONFORD, ESQ.

CONSTITUTION.

ARTICLE I.

SECTION 1.—This Association shall be styled the NEW ORLEANS ACADEMY OF SCIENCES; and its sole object shall be the advancement of Science, properly so called, in all its various departments.

SEC. 2.—The Academy may, in accordance with the powers conferred by its Charter, establish Lectureships in the various Sciences, and also a Library and a Museum, whenever its funds shall admit.

ARTICLE II.

MEMBERSHIP.

SECTION 1.—The New Orleans Academy of Sciences shall consist of the following twenty-seven gentlemen, its founders, viz:

HOWARD SMITH, M. D.
JOSIAH HALE, M. D.
NOAH B. BENEDICT, M. D.
H. D. BALDWIN, M. D.
WM. B. LINDSAY, M. D.
ALBERT W. ELY, M. D.
J. S. COPES, M. D.
J. C. SIMONDS, M. D.
EDWARD C. BOLTON, ESQ.
I. L. CRAWCOUR, M. D., M.R.C.S.E.
D. F. MITCHEL, ESQ.
HENRY HUGHES, ESQ.
PROF. WM. C. DUNCAN, A. M.
PROF. R. H. CHILTON.
W. P. RIDDELL, A. B.
REV. WM. A. SCOTT, D. D.
PROF. J. L. RIDDELL, A. M.,M. D.
REV. ALEX. CAMPBELL, D. D.
ERASTUS EVERETT, A. M.
REV. ISAAC J. HENDERSON.
DUNCAN MACGIBBON, M. D.
BENNET DOWLER, M. D.
PROF. E. H. BARTON, A. M., M. D.
J. M. W. PICTON, M. D.
ALBERT G. BLANCHARD, ESQ., C. E.
CALEB G. FORSHEY, ESQ., C. E.
F. M. CORRY, ESQ.,

and such other gentlemen as may be distinguished for their learning and scientific or literary attainments.

SEC. 2.—The members shall be styled Fellows, Corresponding Members, and Honorary Members, of the New Orleans Academy of Sciences.

SEC. 3.—Every candidate for membership of the Academy, shall be proposed in writing, by three Fellows at least; he shall receive a unanimous vote, except in the case of a single negative to be provided for in the By-Laws; and shall possess the proper moral qualifications: it being *provided*, that, no person shall be eligible to membership until he shall have given proof of his devotion to Science or Literature, by some act of genuine liberality for their advancement, or by the production of a paper on some Scientific or Literary subject. Nominations for membership must lie on the table for one month before a vote can be taken thereon.

SEC. 4.—Gentlemen occupying high positions in the Scientific world, both in this and in other countries, may be elected Honorary Members, or Corresponding Members, by a unanimous vote of the Academy.

SEC. 5.—Honorary members shall have all the privileges of the Academy except the right of voting and of holding office.

SEC. 6.—Corresponding members shall have all the privileges of the Academy except the right of voting and of holding office; and in case of their becoming citizens of New Orleans or vicinity, shall be entitled to Fellowship. It being *provided*, that any Fellow, removing permanently from the city shall, at his option, and on giving due notice to the Academy, become a Corresponding Member.

SEC. 7.—Any member may be expelled for cause, after due hearing and investigation, by a two-thirds vote of the Academy in executive session.

ARTICLE III.

OFFICERS.

SECTION 1.—The Officers of the New Orleans Academy of Sciences, shall consist of a *President*, two *Vice Presidents*, a *Corresponding Secretary*, a *Recording Secretary*, a *Registrar*, a *Treasurer*, a *Librarian*, and two *Curators*; all of whom shall be elected annually.

ARTICLE IV.

MEETINGS: QUORUM.

SECTION 1.—The Academy shall meet at such time and place as may be fixed by the By-Laws.

SEC. 2.—Seven Fellows entitled to vote shall constitute a quorum for the election of officers and new members; for changing the Constitution or By-Laws, as hereinafter provided; and for the appropriation of money. Five Fellows shall constitute a quorum for all other business.

ARTICLE V.

FINANCES.

SECTION 1.—The fee for initiation shall invariably be paid by every Fellow elect, at the time of signing the Constitution; and said fee shall be annually fixed by the Academy.

SEC. 2.—All moneys in the Treasury shall be appropriated to Scientific and other purposes connected with the advancement of the Academy.

SEC. 3.—No money shall be drawn from the Treasury except in accordance with a Resolution of the Academy, on an order signed by the President and countersigned by the Registrar.

ARTICLE VI.

BY-LAWS—AMENDMENTS.

SECTION 1.—Any By-Laws may be made, not inconsistent with this Constitution; which By-Laws may be repealed or amended at any regular monthly meeting, by a vote of two-thirds of the Fellows present; but said By-Laws may be temporarily suspended at any meeting by a two-thirds vote.

SEC. 2.—This Constitution shall be altered or amended only at a regular monthly meeting, and by a unanimous vote of all the Fellows present. A motion to amend must be in writing and lie on the table for one month, during which time it shall be kept posted on the Bulletin board in the hall of the Academy by the Registrar.

BY-LAWS.

ARTICLE I.

ELECTION OF OFFICERS.

SECTION 1.—The annual election of officers shall be held at the first meeting of March of each year; but vacancies may be filled at any other monthly meeting.

SEC. 2.—The Ballot shall be with paper Ballots and a majority shall elect.

SEC. 3.—No Fellow who may be in arrears for dues, shall be entitled to vote, unless by special resolution of the Academy.

ARTICLE II.

DUTIES OF OFFICERS.

SECTION 1.—THE PRESIDENT shall preside at all the meetings of the Academy; shall have a casting vote in case of a tie and not otherwise, except in the election of new members, and on amendments of the Constitution; and shall deliver an *annual address* before the Academy at its last meeting in February.

SEC. 2.—THE VICE PRESIDENTS shall perform the duties of the President in case of his absence.

SEC. 3.—THE CORRESPONDING SECRETARY shall conduct the correspondence of the Academy; and shall preserve copies of all his communications in a book kept for the purpose.

SEC. 4.—THE RECORDING SECRETARY shall keep the minutes of the Scientific proceedings of the Academy, and shall issue notices for special Scientific meetings. He shall also keep a register in which he shall cause to be entered the names of all visitors to the Academy.

It shall be his duty to report all business which may be transacted at the weekly meetings of the Academy, to the Registrar, for incorporation with the executive minutes.

SEC. 5.—THE REGISTRAR shall keep the minutes of the monthly and executive sessions of the Academy in a seperate book; serve all executive notices; keep and affix the Seal of the Academy to all documents requiring authentication. He shall also report to the Recording Secretary, for permanent record, the Donations received, Scientific papers read, and Scientific discussions had, at the monthly meetings.

Sec. 6.—The Treasurer shall keep an accurate account of the receipts and expenditures of the Academy and of the dues of each Fellow, and shall make a report of the state of the treasury, quarterly, or oftener, if required by the Academy. He shall also furnish the Registrar with a list of the qualified voters previous to each election.

Before entering upon his duties the Treasurer elect shall furnish to the President a Bond, with good and solvent securities (either personal, or secured by mortgage at the expense of the Academy;) the amount of which shall be equal to the moneys of the Academy likely to come into his hands the ensuing current year: conditioned upon the faithful performance of his duty. Should the necessity arise during the current year, from donations of money, or otherwise, the Treasurer may be required, under pain of losing the office, to give additional Bonds; so that the funds of the Academy in his keeping may at all times be secured, as contemplated.

Sec. 7.—The Librarian shall take charge of the Library and perform the duties usual to a Librarian.

Sec. 8.—The Curators shall take charge of all apparatus and all real and personal property belonging to the Academy, and make all purchases authorized by the same, unless otherwise provided; they shall also attend to the renting and furnishing of rooms or buildings for the use of the Academy.

Sec. 9.—The President and Registrar shall constitute a standing Committee to audit, semi-annually, the accounts and condition of the treasury, and report thereon to the Academy.

ARTICLE III.

SCIENTIFIC SECTIONS.

Section 1.—For the purposes of Classification, and for facilitating the advancement of Science, the Academy shall be divided into the following Scientific sections, viz:

1. Natural History of Animals.
2. Botany.
3. Geology and Mineralogy.
4. Chemistry and Natural Philosophy.
5. Astronomy and Mathematics.
6. Antiquarian Researches and Ethnology.
7. History and Biography.
8. Philology.
9. Medicine and Physiology.
10. Geography, Statistics and Meteorology.
11. Psychology and Æsthetics.
12. Agriculture.
13. Jurisprudence and Political Economy.

Other Sections may be added when deemed necessary by the Academy.

SEC. 2.—Each Scientific section shall be under the supervision of a Committee of at least three ; the number to be increased as the labors of the section may require. The Chairmen of the several Committees shall be elected annually and shall constitute a Board of Publication.

SEC. 3.—It shall be the duty of the several Committees of Sections to take charge of all papers after their presentation to the Academy, and report them to the Board of Publication.

ARTICLE IV.

MEETINGS.

SECTION 1.—The Academy shall meet every Monday evening at 7½ o'clock from April to September inclusive ; and at 6½ o'clock during the rest of the year. Regular monthly meetings shall be on the first Monday of each month.

SEC. 2.—On request of five Fellows the President shall call a *special executive meeting* ; and on request of three Fellows, a *special* scientific meeting.

SEC. 3.—At special meetings, no business shall be "in order" except that for which the meeting was called.

ARTICLE V.

MEMBERSHIP.

SECTION 1.—The ballot for membership shall be with white and black balls; two black balls always rejecting the candidate. If a single black ball be cast, the ballot shall be repeated, and if a black one still appear, the election shall be suspended until the next regular monthly meeting, when a third ballot shall be taken, and if no more than one black ball still appear, the candidate shall be declared duly elected.

SEC. 2—Every Fellow on being admitted shall sign the Constitution and By-Laws, in a book kept for that purpose ; thereby agreeing to support and abide by the same.

SEC. 3.—Any Fellow failing for twelve months to pay his dues, shall, after one month's notice from the Treasurer, *ipso facto* cease to be a member.

SEC. 4.—In case of charges of gross misconduct against any member of the Academy, the President and the two Vice Presidents shall constitute the Committee of Investigation to report upon the facts.

SEC. 5.—Every member of the Academy shall be considered as having pledged his honor not to divulge any of the transactions of the Academy while in *executive session.*

SEC. 6.—Any gentleman, duly notified of his election as a Fellow of this Academy, who shall fail to subscribe the Constitution within three months, (unless absent from the city during the whole time,) and any gentleman notified of his election as an Honorary Member, or as a Corresponding Member, who shall fail to signify his acceptance within six months, shall be considered as having declined membership.

Diplomas shall be furnished to those Corresponding Members who may desire them, on the receipt of Five Dollars.

ARTICLE VI.

RULES OF ORDER.

SECTION 1.—Business shall be transacted only at the monthly meetings. All intermediate meetings shall be devoted to Scientific labors.

WEEKLY MEETINGS.

SEC. 2.—The order of proceedings at the regular *weekly* meetings shall be as follows:

1st. Reading minutes of previous weekly meeting.
2d. Reception of Donations.
3d. Reading of Communications.
4th. Reading of Scientific Papers.
5th. Verbal communications and miscellaneous discussion.
6th. Adjournment.

MONTHLY MEETINGS.

SEC. 3.—The order of business at the regular *monthly* meetings shall be as follows:

1st. Reading minutes of previous monthly meeting.
2d. Reception of Donations.
3d. Reports of Committees.
4th. Unfinished Business.
5th. New Business.
6th. Elections.
7th. Nominations for Membership.
8th. Scientific communications and discussions.
9th. Adjournment.

SEC. 4.—The Curators' Report shall always be in order.

SEC. 5.—The other rules of order shall be such as are customary in Scientific associations.

ARTICLE VII.

MISCELLANEOUS.

SECTION 1.—No assessment shall be made on the Fellows except by a vote of two-thirds of all present at a regular *monthly meeting;* the rate of assessment for each year shall be fixed in March.

SEC. 2.—No Fellow shall take any book or other publication or property from the hall of the Academy without special leave from the Academy.

SEC. 3.—All papers read before the Academy shall be considered the property of the Academy and shall be filed for preservation.

SEC. 4.—No Fellow shall occupy more than one hour in reading any paper except by permission of the Academy.

SEC. 5.—Public sittings of the Academy may be held at such times and places as the Fellows may determine: the object of such sittings being the delivery of lectures on Scientific subjects.

SEC. 6.—Strangers, or residents of the city may, by *special* invitation of any Fellow, attend the *Scientific* meetings of the Academy; but further than this, such meetings shall not be considered public.

FELLOWS.

A

ABBOTT, A. L.
ANFOUX, Dr. THEOPHILUS
AUCHMUTY, S. P.

B

BAILEY, JAS. K.
BALDWIN, Dr. H. D.
BARBOT, Dr. J. P.
BAYLES, Dr. A. H.
BENEDICT, Dr. N. B.
BLANCHARD, Maj. A. G.
BOLLES, Rev. E. C.
BONFORD, P. E.
BONZANO, Dr. M. F.
BRICKELL, Dr. D. W.
BROWN, W. S.

C

* CAMPBELL, Rev. ALEX.
CARTWRIGHT, Dr. SAM'L A.
CHAPMAN, M. W.
* CHILTON, Prof. R. H.
CLARK, Dr. JOHN S.
CLEGHORN, Rev. E. B.
CLINE, HENRY
COHEN, M. M.
COPES, Dr. J. S.
* COPES, THO. CERRE.
* CORRY, F. M.
CRAWCOUR, Dr. I. L.

D

DE BOW, J. D. B.
DE LANCY, Rev. R. A.
* DUNCAN, GREER B.
DUNCAN, LUCIUS C. Jr.
DURAND, JAMES B.

F

FENNER, Dr. E. D.
FLORAT, J. A.

G

GAYARRE, Hon. CHARLES
GINDER, HENRY
GORDON, WM. ALEX.

H

HARRISON, Prof. J. S.
HUNTER, G. WALLACE

K

KERR, R. C.
KNAPP, Dr. J. S.
KOHLMEYER, Prof. H.
KRUTTSCHNITT, J.

L

LATHAM, LORENZO
LEOVY, HENRY J.
LINDSAY, Dr. WM. B.
LOW, J. H.

M

MACNAIR, JOHN
MEAD, WM. F.
MITCHELL, D. F.
MURRAY, THOMAS

N

NEVITT, A. S.

P

PALMER, Rev. B. M.
PENNISTON, Prof. A., M. D.
PERKINS, W. M.
POLK, Rt. Rev. LEONIDAS
PRIDE, CHARLES

R

RICHARDS, NEWTON
RICHARDSON, Prof. T. G.
RIDDELL, Prof. J. L.
ROGERS, WM. O.

S

SEARS, Prof. C. W.
SKIPWITH, P. H.
SMITH, Dr. HOWARD
SUNDERLAND, Dr. WM. P.

T

THOMAS, HENRY
THOMASSY, RAYMOND
TREFFRY, HENRY W.
TRUDEAU, Dr. JAMES

V

VALLAS, Prof. ANTHONY

W

WAPLES, RUFUS
WHITE, Dr. C. B.

HONORARY MEMBERS.

Prof. LOUIS AGASSIZ, Cambridge University.
Prof. A. D. BACHE, Chief of U. S. Coast Survey.
Prof. JOS. HENRY, Sec. Smithsonian Institute.
*Baron ALEX. VON HUMBOLT, Berlin, Prussia.
*Dr. E. K. KANE, Arctic Navigator.
Lieut. M. F. MAURY, National Observatory.

* Deceased.

CORRESPONDING MEMBERS.

A

ALEXANDER, DR. J. BELL, Mobile, Ala.
ANDREWS, DR. EDWARD, Chicago, Ill.
ARMSBY, PROF. JAS. H., Albany, N. Y.

B

BAIRD, PROF. S. F., Asst. Sec. Smithsonian Inst.
BARLOW, HON. THOS., Canastota, N. Y.
BAYLEY, G. W., Opelousas & G W. R. R., La.
BEADLE, REV. E. R., Hartford, Conn.
BENEDICT, DR. THOS. B., Kirks Ferry, La.
BLACKIE, PROF. GEO. S., Nashville, Tenn.
BLODGET, LORIN, Smithsonian Institution.
BOLTON, DR. E. C., Philadelphia.
BOOTH, PROF. J. C., Franklin Institute, Phila.
BROWN, ANDREW, Natchez, Miss.
BUTLER, DR. S. W., Philadelphia.

C

CAMAK, DR. JAMES, State Line, La.
CARRIGAN, HON. J. N., Baton Rouge, La.
*CASSON, DR. JOHN, San Francisco, Cal.
CHAPMAN, DR. A. W., Apalachicola, Fla.
CHASE, REV. BENJ., Natchez, Miss.
CHAUVEAU, PIERRE J. O., Montreal, C. E.
CHRISTY, PROF. DAVID, Hamilton, Ohio.

D

DILLE, ISRAEL, Newark, Ohio.
DROZ, HENRY, Baton Rouge, La.
DE SAUSSURE, HENRI, Geneva, Switzerland.
DUNGAN, DR. J. B., Jeanerrettes, St. Mary, La.

E

ELLIS, ALEX. JOHN, Bath, England.
ELY, DR. A. W., Washington, D. C.
*ERNST, REV. S. F., Port Hudson, La.
EVERETT, PROF. ERASTUS, Brooklyn, N. Y.

F

FARRAR, DR. S. C., Jackson, Miss.
FORSHEY, PROF. C. G., Rutersville, Texas.
FRAZER, PROF. J. F., Univ. of Pa., Phila.
FRAUENFEL, G., Sec. Zool. & Botan. Soc. of Vienna, Austria.
FRIESACH, DR. CHA'S., Capt. Austrian Army.

G

GOULD, DR. B. A., JR., Albany, N. Y.

H

*HALE, DR. JOSIAH, Canton, Miss.
HALL, DR. HENRY, F., Lewes, Del.
*HALL, DR. MARSHALL, London, England.
HARPER, DR. L., Oxford, Miss.
HART, PROF. JOHN S., Philadelphia, Pa.
HATCH, T. B. R., Lake Providence, La.
HEBERT, LOUIS, State Eng., Baton Rouge, La.
HEERMAN, THEODORE, Wilmington, Del.
HILGARD, J. E., Ass't. U. S. C. Survey, Wash'ton.
HILL, REV. THOMAS, Waltham, Mass.
HODGKIN, DR. THOMAS, London, England.
HUGHES, HENRY, Port Gibson, Miss.

J

JOHNSON, PROF. H. A., Chicago, Ill.

K

KNIGHT, PROF. JONATHAN, New Haven, Ct.
KURSHEEDT, GERSHOM, New York.

L

LA ROCHE, DR. RENE, Philadelphia, Pa.
LATOUR, CAPT. DE L. A. HUGUET, Montreal, C.E.
LINTON, PROF. M. L., St. Louis, Mo.
LOVELACE, DR. P. E. H., Sicily Island, La.

M

MACGIBBON, DR. D., Osyka, Miss.
McCLELLAN, CAPT. GEO., U. S. Top. Engrs.
McGUFFY, REV. W. H., University of Va.
McILVAIN, REV. DR. J. H., Rochester, N. Y.
MAPES, PROF. J. J., New York City.
MASON, HON. CHARLES, Washington, D. C.
MAYER, BRANTZ, Baltimore, Md.
MITCHELL. PROF. O. M., Cincinnati, Ohio.
MORE, PROF. W. D., Oakland College, Miss.

N

NOTT, PROF. J. C., Mobile, Ala.

O

ODLING, DR. WM., Guy's Hospital, London, Eng.
ODOARDO, DON JOSE H., Havana, Cuba.

P

PALMER, PROF. A. B., Ann Arbor, Mich.
PALMER, DR. E., St. James, La.
PITMAN, BENN, Cincinnati, Ohio.
PORTER, DR. J. B., U. S. A., Coventry, Ct.
PROCTOR, DR. STEPHEN, Columbia, Ark.

R

READ, HON. DAVID, Winooski Falls, Vt.
REES, DR. GEO. O., London, Eng.
RIDDELL, DR. WM. P., Austin, Texas.
*ROMER, DR. F. J. B., Baton Rouge, La.

S

SAGER, PROF. ABRAM, Ann Arbor, Mich.
SCHMARDA, PROF. L. K., Univ. Gratz, Austria.
SCHROEDER, ANDREAS, Sec'y. Acad. Science, Vienna, Austria.
SCOTT, REV. W. A., San Francisco, Cal.
SHUMARD, DR. B. F., Austin, Texas.
SIMONDS, DR. J. C., Greensboro, Ala.
SMITH, HON. ASHBEL, Austin, Texas.
SNELL, PEREZ, Sonora, California.

T

TAPPAN, DR. HENRY P., Ann Arbor, Mich.
*TULLY, PROF. WM., Springfield, Mass.
*TUCKERMAN, EDWARD, Amherst, Mass.

V

VINCENT, T. N., Magnolia, Miss.
*VOSBURG, CHARLES, Meridian, Miss.

W

WAILES, COL. B. L. C., Washington, Miss.
WALKER, DR. E. M., Yorktown, Texas.
WARDER, PROF, J. A., Cincinnati, Ohio.
WILSON, PROF. DANIEL, Toronto, C. W.
WILSON, REV. JOHN LEIGHTON, New York.
WILSON, DR. JOHN T. J., Tallahassee, Fla.

Y

YOUNG, DR. C. G., Monroe, La.

*Deceased.

www.ingramcontent.com/pod-product-compliance
Lightning Source LLC
LaVergne TN
LVHW020637110826
845149LV00004B/1237